Put Your Worries Away

by Gill Hasson
illustrated by Sarah Jennings

Published in North America by Free Spirit Publishing Inc., Minneapolis, Minnesota, 2019

Library of Congress Cataloging-in-Publication Data
Names: Hasson, Gill, author. | Jennings, Sarah, illustrator.
Title: Put your worries away / written by Gill Hasson ; illustrated by Sarah Jennings.
Description: Minneapolis : Free Spirit Publishing, 2019. | Series: Kids can cope ; Book 1 | Audience: Age: 6–9
Identifiers: LCCN 2018054296 | ISBN 9781631984310 (hardcover) | ISBN 1631984314 (hardcover)
Subjects: LCSH: Worry—Juvenile literature. | Anxiety—Juvenile literature.
Classification: LCC BF575.W8 H37 2019 | DDC 152.4/6—dc23 LC record available at https://lccn.loc.gov/2018054296

Edited by Alison Behnke and Marjorie Lisovskis

Printed in China

Free Spirit Publishing
An Imprint of Teacher Created Materials
6325 Sandburg Road, Suite 100
Minneapolis, MN 55427-3674
(612) 338-2068
help4kids@freespirit.com
freespirit.com

First published in 2019 by Franklin Watts, a division of Hachette Children's Books · London, UK, and Sydney, Australia

Series editor: Jackie Hamley

Series designer: Cathryn Gilbert

Put Your Worries Away

by Gill Hasson
illustrated by Sarah Jennings

Do you ever worry? Did you know that everybody worries sometimes?

The good news is that you can take charge of your worries and feel better. This book tells you how.

What are worry and anxiety?

Worry and anxiety are thoughts and feelings that can upset you and make you feel bad inside. When you worry, you think something sad or bad might happen and you don't know what to do about it.

Sometimes the things that worry us are real. Sometimes they are things we imagine.

What if my friends won't play with me?

What if our cat runs away again?

What if there's a monster at the door?

If someone comes to pick you up and if your cat doesn't run away, you'll probably stop worrying about those things. But until then, you might think a lot about whatever is worrying you.

How do you feel when you're worried?

Worry and anxiety are not "just in your head." You can feel worries in your body too. Your heart may thump. You might feel butterflies in your tummy. Or your head might hurt.

When you worry, you may feel hot and cold or funny and faint or need to use the bathroom a lot.

Perhaps you tell your mom or dad that your head or stomach hurts.

What do you do when you're worried?

Besides thinking upsetting thoughts and feeling funny, you might not want to go to places or do things when you feel worried. Sometimes you might not want to go to school or even play with your friends.

Sometimes worries can keep you awake at night.
You might feel like you can't sleep on your own.

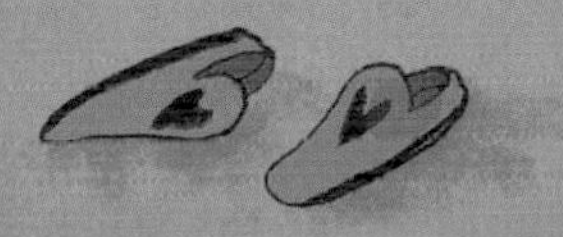

Talking about your worries

When people know that you're worried, they might say things like, "Don't worry about it! Everything will be okay."

Sometimes they might even get upset with you or tell you not to be so silly.

But when people say things like that, it's about as much help to you as a paper raincoat.

In other words, it's not much help at all!

Getting help with your worries

Even if people tell you there's nothing to worry about, or say you're being silly, ***do*** tell someone. Worries are not silly. Don't keep your worries to yourself.

Tell someone you like and trust. Choose a quiet time to talk, and make sure you have the person's full attention.

Say, "I'm worried. Can I talk to you about it?" If the person can't listen to you closely at that moment, plan a time to talk later.

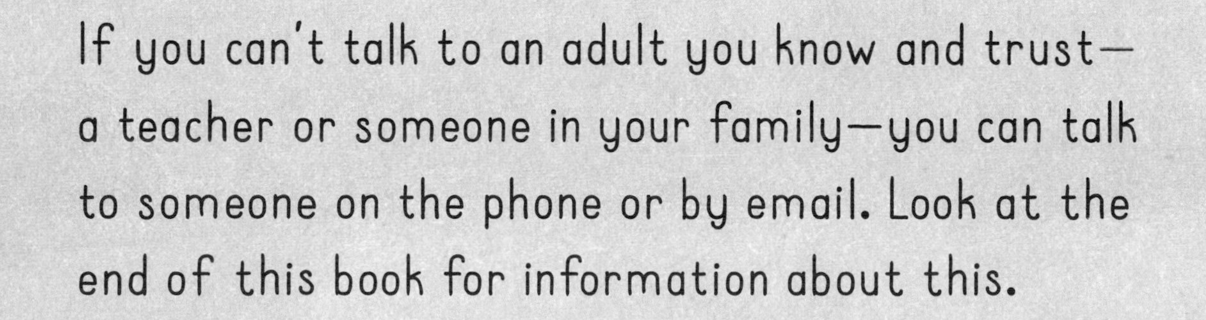

If you can't talk to an adult you know and trust—a teacher or someone in your family—you can talk to someone on the phone or by email. Look at the end of this book for information about this.

What else can you do?

You can change your thoughts and stop the worrying from taking over. Instead of focusing on worrying thoughts, you can concentrate on helpful thoughts.

When you're worried, the part of your brain that thinks sad, scary thoughts takes control. It stops the sensible, helpful part of your brain from working for you.

This means that when you're worried, your brain has no room for helpful thoughts.

What if my dad gets sick?

What if nobody likes me?

So, the first thing to do is to calm down. That way, the sensible part of your brain can work and make space for helpful thoughts.

Change your thoughts

You can do lots of things to move your mind away from worrying thoughts and make room for calmer, more helpful thoughts. Here are just a few ideas:

Count to four as you breathe in. Then count to four as you breathe out. Breathe like this 10 times.

Count backward from 30.

Breathe in like you're smelling the scent of a flower. Then breathe out like you're blowing bubbles.

Sing a song.

Remember everything you had to eat and drink yesterday.

Nico feels worried about joining a new club. Everyone says he will enjoy it, but he still feels nervous the night before. To stop feeling so worried, he does his best to remember a good time—a party or a day out. He tries to remember all the different nice things that happened.

What other ideas do you have?

Instead of worrying

Once you've moved worrying thoughts out of the way, you can have helpful thoughts. You can start to think about how to deal with what's worrying you.

Beth was worried that her dad would be late picking her up from soccer practice and that she'd be left at the gym all by herself.

They made a plan. "If I think I'll be late," said Beth's dad, "I'll text your soccer coach to let him know. And I'll phone your friend Yasmin's mom and ask her to pick you up."

"Thanks," said Beth. "I feel better now that we have a plan."

Make your own plan

Is there something you're worried about right now? What is it?

If you can, ask someone else—a grown-up or a friend—to help you make a plan to deal with what's worrying you.

When you've made your plan, picture each part of your plan in your mind.

You might remember your plan and keep it in your head.

Or you could write down your plan or draw it.

Once you have a plan, if a worry comes into your head again, tell yourself: "Stop! I have a plan!"

Put your worries away

Sometimes, you might not be able to think of a plan. What can you do then? There are some worries that you cannot plan away. But you could try putting your worries away or even giving them away.

To put your worries away, write down or draw what you're worried about. Then fold up the piece of paper and put it in a box, a drawer, a jar, or a small bag.

Or you could give away your worries to a toy or to your dog, cat, rabbit, or hamster. Tell them what you're worried about. Knowing someone else has heard your worry can help it feel less scary. Then let them worry for you.

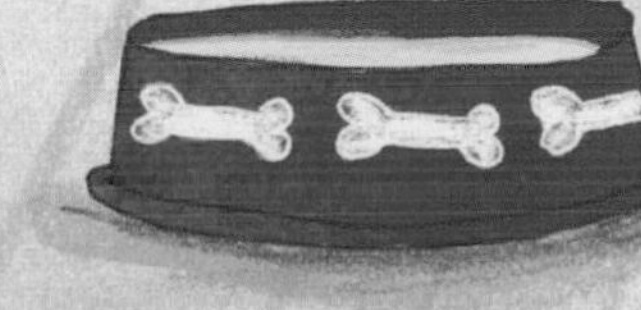

Take a break from worrying!

Once you've put away or given away your worries, you can do other things to give yourself a break from worrying. You can do something you enjoy so there's less room in your mind for anxious thoughts.

Here are some ideas:

drawing, painting or coloring . . .

making or building something . . .

doing a puzzle or playing a game . . .

reading a book or watching a movie . . .

playing with your friends,
your dog, or your cat . . .

kicking a ball, riding your bike, or
just running around in circles . . .

singing and dancing to music.

Tell the worry to go away

If a worry pops up in your mind even while you're doing something else, you can say, "Go away! I'm busy right now." Then go back to the nice thing that you were doing.

You can do better things with your time than worry. So when you notice that anxious thoughts are swirling in your head, do something else. Do something that makes it difficult for worries to take over.

Put worries away at bedtime

If you feel worried when it's time to go to bed, you can give your mind something else to think about—something nice. Ask if you can read a book or listen to music or a story. Or, in your head, go to your own happy place.

To do that, think of something comforting or funny that once happened to you—something that makes you feel good when you think about it.

Remember as much as you can: What did you do? Who was with you? What did you talk about? What was the weather like? What did you wear? You can create as many happy places for yourself as you like!

Put Your Worries Away

Now you know what worry and anxiety are. They're thoughts and feelings that upset you and distract you. You can feel them in your body too. But you *can* do things to cope with them. Here are some reminders:

- Get the helpful part of your brain to start working again so that you do something about what's worrying you.
- Make a plan to deal with what's worrying you.
- Put your worry away or give it away.
- Give yourself a break from worrying by doing something you enjoy.
- If the worry comes back while you're doing something else, tell it to "go away!"

When a worry feels too big to handle, ask a grown-up for help. If you do not feel you can ask anyone you know, you can call **1-800-448-3000**, text **CONNECT** to **741741**, or go to **yourlifeyourvoice.org** to talk with a counselor. This person will listen to you and give you some help and advice about what to do if you're worried about something.

Activities

These drawing and writing activities can help you think more about how to handle your worries. You could keep your pictures and writing with this book so that you have your own ideas about how to cope when you're worried.

- Draw or write about something you're worried about.
- Draw a picture of yourself. Color in the parts of your body that don't feel good when you're worried.
- Micah is worried about a spelling test next week. He's worried there will be lots of words that he doesn't know how to spell. What do you think Micah could do about it? Write a letter to Micah with some advice and some kind words.
- Nadia is worried that when she and her sister go to the park tomorrow, their friends won't let them join in and play with them. Can you think of a plan for Nadia and her sister? Draw them a picture with ideas for what they could do.
- Write out a plan to deal with something you are worried about. Draw some pictures of yourself in each part of your plan.
- Draw a picture of things you like doing that can give you a break from your worries.
- Write down the sort of things you can tell yourself if, while you're doing something else, a worry does pop up in your mind. Draw a picture of yourself telling yourself these things.
- Write down happy thoughts you could focus on instead of worrying. Draw pictures of some happy times you've had. For each happy time, remember as much as you can: What did you do? Who was with you? What did you talk about? What was the weather like? What did you wear?

Notes for teachers, parents, and other adults

If you care for a child who worries—whether it's about one thing or lots of things—you'll know that simply telling children "don't worry" or trying to reassure them by saying "there's nothing to worry about" just doesn't work.

When you are worried or anxious, your worries feel very real to you. It's the same for children—their worries exist as fact. Even if they're worrying about something that does not exist—like monsters or other imaginary creatures—their worry is still real.

Put Your Worries Away starts by acknowledging this. The first few pages describe the kinds of worries children might have, how worrying can feel, and the sorts of things children might do in response to their worries.

Although children can read this book by themselves, it will be more helpful for both of you if you read it together. Talk with children about the sort of worries they might have. Ask them how they feel and what they do when they're worried. You might have stories to share from your own childhood about something you worried about.

Children need effective techniques and strategies to help them take control and feel in charge of worry and anxiety. ***Put Your Worries Away*** explains ways children can manage their worries, providing a range of strategies you can help them with: making a plan to deal with what's worrying them, ideas for taking a break from worrying, suggestions for how to put their worries away, and ways to tell their worries to go away.

Some children might want to read this book all at once. Others will find it easier to manage and understand a few pages at a time. Either way, you'll find plenty to talk about with children. Ask them questions and provide prompts such as: "Have you ever tried that?" "What do you think of that idea?" "How could that work for you?" Talk about the characters in the illustrations.

After reading the book and helping children identify strategies that could work for them, you can come back to the book often to remind yourselves of ways to handle any future worries.

With time, patience, support, and encouragement from you, children will learn to cope with and overcome their worries. But if their anxiety is frequently causing them distress and leading them to avoid everyday situations and miss out, it's worth seeking more advice. Reach out to a healthcare provider, counselor, or other expert and ask for help.